GREAT TALES FROM LONG AGO

JOAN OF ARC

Retold by Catherine Storr
Illustrated by Robert Taylor

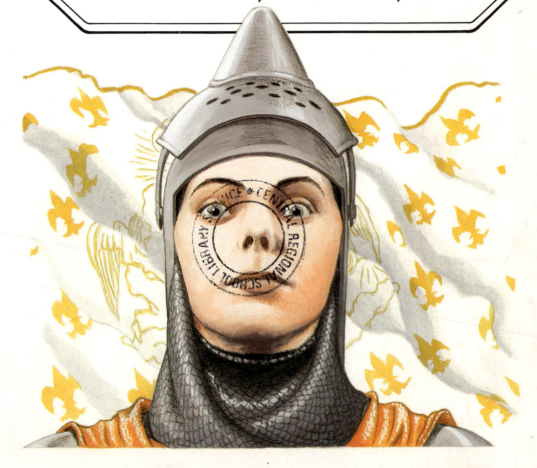

Methuen Children's Books
in association with Belitha Press Ltd.

F

Note: The text and illustrations
are based on authentic
historical sources, and on *Joan
of Arc* by Marina Warner,
London 1981.

ED.

Copyright © in this format Belitha Press Ltd., 1985
Text copyright © Catherine Storr 1985
Illustrations copyright © Robert Taylor 1985
Art Director: Treld Bicknell
First published in Great Britain 1985
by Methuen Children's Books Ltd.,
11 New Fetter Lane, London EC4P 4EE
Conceived, designed and produced by Belitha Press Ltd.,
2 Beresford Terrace, London N5 2DH
ISBN 0 416 49170 7 (hardback)
ISBN 0 416 49600 8 (paperback)
Printed in Hong Kong by South China Printing Co.

More than five hundred years ago the French and the English were fighting each other. Large parts of France were already ruled by England. When King Henry of England had married Katherine, a French princess, it was agreed that their son should be King of all France, as well as King of England.

RHEIMS

PARIS

ORLEANS VAUCOULEURS

CHINON

DOMREMY

FRANCE

N

A T THIS TIME, A FARMER CALLED D'ARC
lived with his family in the little village
of Domrémy, near the north of France.
The farmer had three sons and a daughter,
called Jeanne, or Joan.
Joan seemed to be an ordinary young girl.
She worked in the house with her mother,
and sometimes she helped her father on his farm.

THERE WERE NO VILLAGE SCHOOLS IN THOSE DAYS,
so Joan never learned to read or write.
She spent most of her time
praying in the village church.
Joan thought that she heard the voices
of Saint Margaret, Saint Catherine and Saint Michael.
They told her that she had been chosen
to go to war to save the Kingdom of France.

SHE WENT HOME AND TOLD HER FATHER
that she must leave the village
and become a soldier,
to save France from the English.
Her father was angry.
"Girls do not ride to war.
Stay at home and do your work here," he said.
"If I hear any more of this nonsense
I shall tell your brothers to drown you."

But Joan would not listen. "No, father.
I am chosen to beat the English
and see our young Prince crowned
in the cathedral of Rheims," she said.

AS HER FATHER WOULD NOT HELP HER,
Joan persuaded a cousin, who made wheels and carts,
to go with her to the castle of a lord
called Baudricourt. Joan wanted him to give her a horse
and some men to accompany her
on the long ride to Chinon
where the young Prince was living.

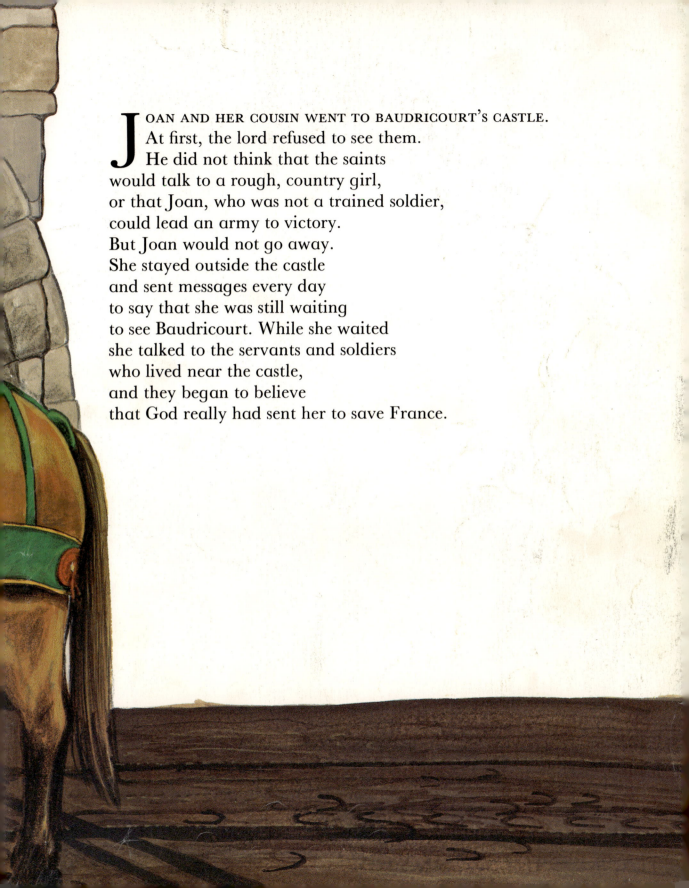

JOAN AND HER COUSIN WENT TO BAUDRICOURT'S CASTLE.
At first, the lord refused to see them.
He did not think that the saints
would talk to a rough, country girl,
or that Joan, who was not a trained soldier,
could lead an army to victory.
But Joan would not go away.
She stayed outside the castle
and sent messages every day
to say that she was still waiting
to see Baudricourt. While she waited
she talked to the servants and soldiers
who lived near the castle,
and they began to believe
that God really had sent her to save France.

A T LAST BAUDRICOURT ALLOWED JOAN
to come inside the castle and to talk to him.
At first he thought she must be mad.
But in the end he saw
that she believed so much in her story
that she might be able
to put new heart into the French army.

He gave her a horse
and some men to guard her
and she set out to ride southwards
to the great river Loire and the castle of Chinon.

BEFORE SHE REACHED CHINON,
Joan went to the shrine of St. Catherine of Fierbois.
Until it was discovered fifty years before Joan came there,
this shrine had been completely hidden by a thick forest.
After she had left Fierbois, Joan's voices told her
that there was a sacred sword hidden in the chapel
which she was to have.
Joan sent messengers to the shrine,
and they found a rusty sword hidden behind the altar.
When the rust was rubbed off,
Joan saw five crosses engraved on the blade.
This was the sword she loved best for the rest of her life.

T HE PRINCE HEARD THAT A YOUNG GIRL
had come all the way from the north,
saying that she could save France,
and crown him as King,
he was not sure whether to believe her or not.
To test her, he ordered one of his nobles
to pretend to be the Prince
when Joan came into the throne room.

He, the real Prince, stood among the crowd.
But directly Joan entered the room
she recognised the Prince.
She knelt down before him and said,
"My lord Prince,
I have been sent by God and the blessed saints
to free our fair country of France from the enemy,
and to see you crowned King at Rheims."

The Prince was pleased
that she had known him in spite of his pretence.
He agreed to give Joan an army
and a horse for her to ride at the army's head.
He also gave her a suit of armour and a sword.
Joan rode out with Dunois, one of the French nobles,
to raise the siege of the city.
With the army went cartloads of provisions
for the starving people of Orleans.

THE ENGLISH FORTS WERE ON THE SOUTH
and the west of Orleans.
So Joan and Dunois led the army
along the river on the other side.
Afterwards, Dunois told how the wind
had been against them, so they could not cross the river.
Suddenly, the wind changed, and they were able to cross
and enter the city.
Dunois thought that this was a miracle.

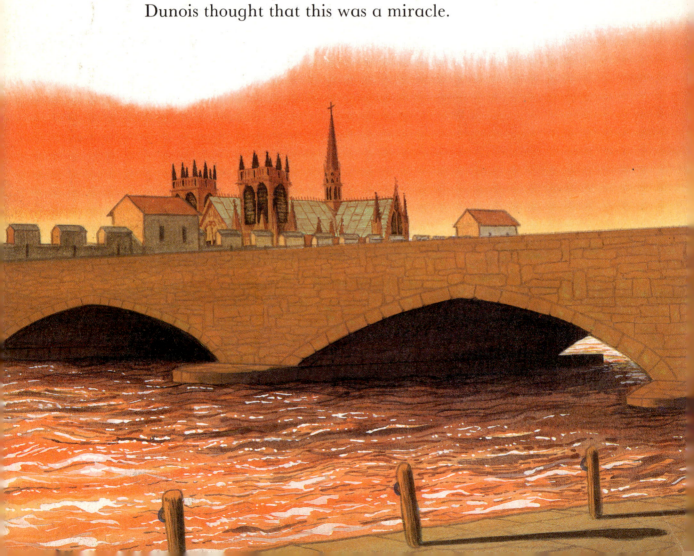

AFTER A FEW DAYS,
Joan and her soldiers came out of the city
to attack the English again.
The battle lasted more than a whole day.
At one moment
an arrow struck Joan's throat, and she fell.

The English were sure she had been killed,
so when they saw her come back
and go on fighting, they believed this was magic
and that Joan was a witch.
They were terrified of witchcraft.
They set fire to the forts
they had built round the city, and left.

J OAN WENT ON TO WIN SEVERAL MORE BATTLES,
and at last the Prince agreed to go to Rheims.
It was a dangerous journey.
The Prince had many enemies among his own countrymen,
as well as among the English.
But they arrived safely
and, in the Cathedral of Rheims,
the Archbishop crowned him
as King Charles the Seventh of France.
At the coronation Joan stood near to the King,
and now she knew that she had done everything
that her voices had told her.

JOAN WANTED TO TAKE PARIS BACK FOR THE FRENCH,
and to defeat the Burgundians and English there.
She led an army to the city,
but they lost the battle, and she was wounded.
Though she was not taken prisoner,
no one helped her to escape.
She had many enemies in the King's court
and not many friends.
The nobles were jealous of her favour with Charles.
The priests of the Catholic Church
thought that God spoke to them
but not to ordinary people, like Joan.
"You are proud and headstrong," they said.

SOON AFTER HER FAILURE AT PARIS
Joan rode to another battle.
She was pulled off her horse by a Burgundian soldier,
and taken prisoner.
After many months in prison,
she was handed over to the French.
During this time, Charles, King of France,
might have tried to rescue Joan.
But her enemies persuaded him
to leave her to her fate.

W HILE JOAN WAS IN PRISON
she was constantly asked questions.
Priests of the Church wanted her to say
that the voices she had heard
had not come from God or his Saints
but from the devil.
If she would not say this
she would be burned as a witch.

This frightened Joan so much
that she agreed she must have been mistaken.
But then she discovered
that, although she could save herself from burning,
she would be kept in prison
for the rest of her life.
When she knew this she tore up her confession.

"I cannot live without the light of day
and freedom. My voices spoke truly to me," she said.
After this, nothing could save her.
She was taken to the market place of Rouen,
tied to a stake and burned to death as a witch.

LATER, BOTH THE FRENCH AND THE ENGLISH
realised what a terrible thing they had done.
The French people saw
that Joan had come to save their country
when it was nearly lost to them.
They put a statue of Joan in Rouen,
and four hundred years later,
the Pope declared that she had not been a witch
nor had she anything to do with the devil.
He said she had been a saint,
and he named her, Saint Joan of Arc.